Both/And

Both/And

William Irwin

WISDOM/WORK
Published by Wisdom/Work
Wilmington, North Carolina

Published 2021

ISBN 9781737722700

Printed in the United States of America

Set in Adobe Garamond Pro
Designed by Abigail Chiaramonte

Contents

Preface

The stanzas we study in English class sometimes speak to us, but they often remain aloof like kids in clubs we can't join. At sixteen it was great therapy, not great art, when I scrawled my feelings on notebook pages. The lines, alas, were so unlike those in *The Norton Anthology* that I soon ditched my plans to become a poet. Sour grapes perhaps, but ideas and insights attracted me more than rhymes and meters. So in college I flirted with psychology and married philosophy. It's been a happy union, yet I've always wanted to do more with words.

Philosophy and poetry are ancient rivals, but they are not competitors in a zero-sum game. In fact, my favorite poetry is philosophical, and my favorite philosophy is poetic—but none of it is accessible. So in this book I've tried to make what I couldn't find, accessible philosophical poetry. Each poem can be read at a glance, and some lines may be worth another look.

literary logic

truish
false but
true enough
like your taxes

falsish
true but
not true enough
like your profile pic

know thyself
if you don't have a problem
then there is no solution

rivalry reconciled
poetry could be philosophy
in a subjunctive mood

eudaimonia
in this effluent
flow-filled flourishing
all things once dammed up
now come easily

to provoke thought
cull a couple of
quarrelsome books

education
out of the cave
know you don't know

not unsafe
meet me
in the open space
where
outrageous opinions
are OK

instructor needed
Defense Against
the Dark Arts
of Newspeak

mission philosophical
to disturb
the falsely
comforted
to comfort
the falsely
disturbed

literary logic
poems don't
prove anything
just change
your mind

free will
is God-like power
to be uncaused
too much to ask?

at gunpoint
free will
will not
leave you

without will power
all the free will
in the world
will leave you
on the couch

freedom
determined
individuals
transcend
fate of
social science

defying determinism
not the sum
of my statistics
neither are you
we fly free
accepting
responsibility

who can tell?
dis-mis-dys
information

intuitive smell
a nose for bullshit
sniffs beyond logic
to learn lies

truth teller
balances beliefs
on the scale
of your mind

useful fictions
pretty illusions
spark in the dark
get you through
but can't be true

human nature
don't look in metaphysical space
for what is written in DNA

nightmare thoughts
skeptical dreams
make cat naps and
doggy slumbers
seem uncertain

epistemological comfort
do not worry dear philosopher
the truth about reality is
metaphysical emergencies
are just illusions and confusions

reality sucks
it shouldn't be so but
beauty is not truth

thinking again and changing your mind
with epistemic humility
even though you love to hold them tight
beliefs degrees of uncertainty
let them go after losing the fight

sins
hypocrisy is human
sanctimony is satanic

safe bet
I predict that
people will never realize
how bad they are
at making predictions

headache formula
complexity
without
justification

Ockham's plea to bureaucrats
do not multiply
(sub)committees
beyond necessity

metaphysics
the furniture
of the universe
is mostly imagined

against Plato
real numbers
are as imaginary
as $\sqrt{-1}$

two worlds or one
do dreaming dogs
understand
when they wake?

against eugenics
even a bad idea
may birth a good one

serendipity
in search of ideas
found philosophy
looking at poetry

random Ridley
when ideas have sex
we all come

no bullshit
quiet man
listens loud

own voice
will not sell
opinions
for praise

unreal
in a phoney world
text messages count
as conversation

de-conform
fight to become
who you are
digging the tunnel
out of their prison
one spoonful at a time

authentic life
dishonesty
is death to me

no exit
other people
can't live with them
can't live without them

non, la nausée
no clutter
in a tree
abundance
without
apology

5 shots fired
96° sun
blares like
boombox
blinding
boys on
beach below

time
poem costs
a penny
pays
a dime

who's in charge?
thought I
was steering
but words and actions
didn't obey
the joystick
in mind

forking paths
a blade of grass
out of place
causes a butterfly
to flap its wings
so why worry
which way to walk?

miniverse
forget the forking paths
we're just a teardrop
in the eye of a beast

Epicurus meets Marx
forget the gods
for they are
fictions and
addictions

altruist?
he did it all
for the dopamine

true
the written word
is a lie

what Alice told the rabbit
to be always never late
make sure to arrive on time

Zarathustra's sense
the poets lie too much?
sure
but we're honest about it

Freudian conspiracy
an accidental
"reply all"
on purpose
who knows?

performative utterance
I
declare
moral
bankruptcy

insight
reason has tools
that logic
knows not of

experience is the real payoff
please don't be misled by mere metaphor
the Pragmatism of William James doesn't say
the cash-value of an idea has
a clear monetary equivalent

save the world
time travel
kill Hegel
in his crib

Nietzsche
his metaphysical violence
caused the death of God

postmodernism
no theory
explains it all

Baudrillard
in the desert of the real
the original copy
was itself a simulacrum

final judgment
Derrida's
différance
does deserve
deriding

life itself
philosophy can't feel
true fiction makes it real

broken beauty
where glue grows weak
we face fractures
of fragile life

identity crisis
life story
comes apart
when facts don't
fit the plot

the linguistic turn

literally
nothing
is wrong
with nihilism

litter
a letter
means
a lot

r
the librarian's
archival archrival
found the letter

a garble
anagrams
make math
ars magna

exclusion
language games
aren't so fun
when you can't play

can't live without
poem is
puzzle piece
unmissing
now needed

loaded disjunction
are you
begging the question
or
stealing the answer?

unity
with all the love
for 'or' and 'of'
'both' joins
from above

linguistic
twins can
be repaired
triplets cannot

words worth little
emotion recollected
in tranquility
pride depicted
in humility

labels lie
call yourself a
virgin porn star
or neo-Hegelian
philatelist
for all I care

(re)capitulate
to surrender
or
to summarize

classical ignorance
Latin to her
was
Greek to me

curse of knowledge
asked for help
computer geek
but he tried
to teach me
in ancient Greek

tone
your words
are bad breath
to the nose
of my ears

no glass
my open window policy
is not an invitation but
I'll gladly throw you out

confused
do little things mean a lot
if you
don't sweat the small stuff?

question of clichés
mending fences
forces water
under the bridge?

professor's paradox
can a charlatan
suffer from
impostor syndrome?

misleading silence
we don't tell
so don't ask
about
secrets hidden
in the plain sight
of normalcy

into success

warning
manage time
or it will
mangle you

no excuses
take hutzpah pill
add attitude
to moxie mix
and get shit done

experiment
in life's lab
fail small
fail often
fail quickly
until you fail
into success

the moment
clock can't tell you
what time it is

niche innovate
write the rules
for your arena
make others
struggle to compete
where your skillset
won't be beat

career counseling
make them pay
for your métier

habit's hammer
final strike
sunders stone
lightning gone
thunder alone

anti-fragile
infect me
stronger

scar display
pain has no claim
to your brain
deal and heal
don't hide the
suffering inside

seize the dawn
do what's
hard
while it's
early

please pause
between stimulus
(is the eternity to decide)
and response

arrive on time
vague plans
don't get
specific results

ad-lib
a routine
self-imposed
is not opposed
to freedom
in deviation

truth hunt
find where
people are right
even when
they're wrong

prudence
disagree
with grace
so she can
save face

humanity
it's crucial
to be kind
and might help
to be blind

helping vampires
no good deed
goes unpunished

unknowns
he didn't know
that you don't know
what you don't know

Homer twist
me, myself, and I
the causes of
and solutions to
all life's problems

childish thing
feels don't
make reals
fair is fiction

who can tell?
leap of faith
or
dive of deception

be still
undaunted
yet
unsure
inaction
won't do

respire restore
inhale deeply
when besieged
exhale deeply
feel relieved

confidence
thank God for
stupidity
who would dare
without it?

recording studio
urgency
induced
creativity

my impression
can't get in?
create your own
salon

add value
take away
delay

remember the future
actions
without
anticipation
of recollection
lack satisfaction

fatal flaw
your planning
doesn't include
what you
don't see

unlucky?
luck takes
the smarts
to know it
when you see it

invisible hand of happiness

day and night
wear the world
like a loose garment
and disrobe for bed
to dream away dread

time balance
make life
easier later
without
wishing
away
time now

time cure
feeling happy?
don't worry
that'll go away

unfactfully
honest anger
true problem
when it lies

let old ways die
tyranny
of yesterday
bullies boys
into anger
today

power
serving with dignity
surpasses
waiting with pride

active silence
loving
listening
requires
restraint
replying

world of opportunity
it didn't
have to happen
but here we are

spiration
breathe in
to remove
myself mentally
from mayhem
breathe out
to include
myself emotionally
in peace

chop wood
life inside
the mind
is enough
to make
you mad

life
bathe in the blue sky
while its water is warm

ego trap
save yourself
from destruction
by escaping
self-absorption

off the rails
mind the gap
between
trains of thought

obsessive thoughts
mental chatter
gets stuck on what
does not matter

take note of little things
sincere gratitude grows
with daily deposits
and compound interest

Dao
less said
is more

om
not all
syllables
are created
equal

fullness of being
branches touching sky
roots digging earth
just me and this tree
would be enough

enjoy being
in the stream
of your
inescapable thought
awash in a
solitary swim

Jack's faith
sincere in astonishment
cherishing you to become
who you are

blackbird has spoken
in love
with the mystery of Being
layers above
what eyes and intellect perceive

just wait
patient
cunning karma
collects and pays
despite delays

Dao FM
signal moves
adjust dial
to stay tuned

blessing
cherish
chance
to be
bored

mudita
without envy
without pride
I share the joy
you feel inside

com-joy
cannot be
happy *for* you
that's impossible
but can be
happy *with* you
that's mudita

math of joy
mudita multiplies
my happiness
by yours

exponential growth
invisible hand
of happiness
delivers
compound interest
on investments
in joy of others

contact
to get high
on life
inhale the joy
of others

happiness increases
unlimited growth
happens when
scarcity mentality
ceases

master peace
worry less
forgive more

commands
make joy
take pride
find fun
eyes wide

present tense?
exercise
meditate
socialize

catch it
in baby bliss
grandma beaming
with
contagious joy

inter-being
always a next you
can't clean plate
of karmic residue

eyes, ears, noses, hands, and tongues

use imagination
sapient savoring
needs mental flavoring

food foreplay
eyes, ears, nose, and hands
mouth is last to eat

sounds easy
sing a song
without words

mom with little kids
you've become nose blind
to food you can't find
rotting in the couch
and stinking behind

Kool-Aid caution
take a
proper gander
before you
cause pain
putting podcast
poison in
your ear
to shut off
your brain

smell past taste
don't settle
for a morsel
of memory

taboo
starts as precaution
becomes
prohibition

hear me
just because
you're loud
doesn't mean
I'm listening

talkers
don't want to be
in their heads
and don't care
what's in yours

introvert power
the quiet one
fears not silence

private I
with unseen eyes
felt watching
realize hedge hid him
from neighbor's HI's

looked at
sunglasses
could not
stop
the stare

forget faces
read minds with feet
the most honest part
of the body
tapping anticipation
jumping for joy
turning to flee

unpredictable
sane mind
can't read
mad man

effort
writer's block
requires
elbow grease
for brain

open sesame
reader's block
can't break
book spine

imperfect appreciation
unsightly
but endearing
and unfixed

declutter
KonMari
bids
res adieu

thank you for your service
poor Post-it® Note
who played placeholder
your glue is gone but
you are not forgotten

dark magic?
paperclip pairings
occur
overnight

people you may know

RIP Jimmy
gay b/4 it was cool
punk rock record store clerk
all recommendations
no regrets

true story
cop asks drunk teenager
in back of cruiser—
what do you wanna be
when you grow up?
a poet I said

a Jew for Jesus
Bob Dylan
bardic
not
Sephardic

patent clerk
spacetime
in
spare time

J. Alfred
not did dare
did descend
the stair

47

know thyself
well-liked Loman
took touchdown
as omen

life of a sailsman
after fleeting
euphoria the
wind goes out
of his sale and
he needs the next
commission high

Frost's bite
golden goddess
astride the field
of hockey
fixed in memory
fading already

Dad
for the fresh cut grass
reminds me of you
as hay fever tears
itch my eyes
and I wonder
at a watch
that keeps ticking

dissonance in dunderland
Michael sometimes believed
as many as
6 conflicting things
before breakfast

Jim loves Pam
with her head
asleep on shoulder
must move to end
the moment
you wish could last

Anthony
he is a poem—
breaking the rules
that don't apply to him
if he says so

Harvard
he's on his way
but did he choose
where to go?

busy man
perpetual
unimportant
motion machine
nothing but
annoying

busybody
only response
to his irksome
little existence
was ignore-ance

bubble boys
positive infection
factory
usually yields
prophets of boom

he can't be trusted as your friend
enemy of your enemy
is probably a bad person

insecure egomaniac
actor didn't get applause
now aggrieved without cause

innovator
open-minded and wide-eyed
through every window Seymour
a possibility spied

outcaste
nicotine yellow
fingers
smoking leper
lingers on
fringes

Simeon says
the famous
unknown hermit
took a public
permanent vacation

political divas
toxic Tina
drawn to drama
picks a fight with
lawn-sign Lana

aggrieved
elder statesman
denied courtesy
of consultation
licks his wounds
amidst the ruins

angry eyes
pock marked chapters
lead to the chair
an alpha male
meets his omega

manic Renee
as Ferris wheel
sees a sinking sun
her world of sushi mountains
and dragons is revealed
through a Motrin respite

imperfectionist
Alexander
the late
conquered
the need
to be great

Cliff Burton
to make such sounds
took bell bottom charm
that would trip no alarm

praise for Parton
it ain't easy
to be trashy
like Miss Dolly

real people
New Yorkers who
have never seen
eponymous
anti-maga zine

monotone Tom
five minutes feels
like forever
when he's talking

untrustworthy colleague
his kind intentions are
nefarious at best

the philosopher
in manspread mindset
scatter my many
metaphysical
theories around

lovely Liz
too unweird
to make it
in showbiz

popular kid
just his season
he's well-liked for
no good reason

secular saint
creating sacred rules of math
was his public act of prayer

janitor
slippery
textured
life of toil

unfunny Fred
likes a good laugh
but can't give one

3rd rate professor
arrogant without cause
pretentious without pause

bus boy
tireless worker
has to get wheels

dead man walking
it's over but not complete
as long as he's moving feet

ideal employee
often on time
seldom inebriated
rarely stole
more than needed

plain sight suffering
the loneliest
popular kid
couldn't break
the bubble
in which he hid

devotee of dullness
senses synchronous snoring
enthralled by all things boring

didn't need the spot
passive aggressive
Pete put it in park
and stayed after dark

with wavering voice
untrusty Paul
fooled
no one at all

places we've been

grandma's house
scents spark
sense of
first-personal
nostalgia

Wilkes-Barre
the gray dome
sucks spirit
but in backyards
of meaningless little houses
touch football
makes everything count

picture Pennsyltucky
underpants
on display
fishing license
pinned to ballcap
redneck rapper
chewin' tobacco
spittin' rhymes

New York
even the lonely
can't be alone

concrete jungles
in cities
real trees
look fake

Yonkers
sure as dogs
do bark
all roads
lead to
Central Ave.
sans the park

Fordham Station
a rat
how appropriate
on the track

Texas
clock says
100° at 12:00 AM
time for some silver dollar pancakes
with plenty of syrup and AC

in that spot
was pleasant
coffee company
no more

land of grace
the king says
snow don't stay
in Memphis

no country for young children
New York, Chicago, Philly …
inner city anywhere
dangerous place to be safe

animals like us

my best friend in bed
soothing snoring from
warm furry body
nestled next to me
dogness brings on sleep

about to strike
seen no sign
heard no word
of diving bird

death from above
when a hawk
takes a puppy
from your backyard
that's a bad day

animal emotions
a rat scurries
without shame
while
a lion reclines
with pride

parrotty
imitation of life
no comprehension
an unintentional
parody

eat with eyes
rabbit splayed
on a plate
looks like rat
on the table

porcupine
your we
doesn't
speak
for me

limits learned
frustrated joy
of a puppy
crashed into
wall of despair

through the year

gray grit
bad cigar
dead lighter
and
broken umbrella
in the rain
just keeps walking …

spring melts
the ugly season
of snow stained
by dog piss
and car exhaust

winter's April
gray
sunless
day

sun rumor
a little hope
as the sky turns
a lighter brighter
shade of gray

Buffalo May
spring finals
in winter jackets

open window
air is fresh
sleep is deep

mind bombs
sunshine
is chocolate
for eyes

vitamin D-joy
with tingle of
sun on skin
photosynthesis
can begin

June 21
tonight
some mania
might be
right

July
after the fireworks
comes the quiet
as ease sets in
stress goes out

under a tree
drinking hot tea
in the summer rain

common summertime cold
I caught a sunburn in the shade
a desert in the glade

augury in August
constant crickets calling
singing strains of
summer's cessation
dog days' demise

forehear
wind whispers
leaves crisp
with sounds
to fall

not meant to last
sun
undone
cumulus
clouds
fracture
fragile
blue
sky

chance encounter
like a doe
on a forest path
see the sunshine
soon gone

above ground
dare to touch a leaf
while you can
feel between fingers
alive on a tree

caffeine curve
less daily sunlight
more tea appetite

taste November
smell of decay
accents
visual dampness
of soaking leaves
magnifying chill

the brown season
leafless trees
colorless grass
sunless sky
Thanksgiving
with pseudo-relatives
in a hotel
near the prison

light snow
more than
nothing
less than
something

winter cotton
silence of snow
absorbing sound
lets you listen
to quiet ground

winter always wins
a glimmer of light
but there is no hope

the hammer of a god
as I winter
out the backdoor
thunderous cold
claps me like Thor

shovlin' done
winter comes knockin'
and ya gottsta pay
the snowman

thanks and goodbye

made peace with it
the war within
my head
won't be won 'til
I'm dead

(un)finished
to end without being complete
is that all there is to a life?

cozy monuments
grandma's afghans will
outlive my poems

communion
poet seeks a publisher
but needs a reader
to take him home

Acknowledgements

Though I sat alone as I wrote these poems, other voices kept me company. The sources of inspiration and support are too many to list. So I'll mention just a few. Jack McSherry, S.J. first encouraged me to write poetry in high school, and he told me not to care about whether it looked or sounded like what I read in *The Norton Anthology*. For years Jack was the only person I would allow to read my poems. He believed in me and helped me to believe in myself. These days Megan Lloyd is my first and best reader, as well as my first and best (and only) wife. Her ear and eye for poetry saved me from some silly mistakes (the ones that remain are all my fault, as most things are). My children, Daniel and Kate, have both taken an interest in my writing and have even offered helpful feedback. I'm fortunate to have such a wonderful family.

Tom Morris never stops thinking about bringing philosophy to a wider audience. His legendary lectures and bestselling books have reached millions. I am deeply grateful to him for his philosophical evangelism and for the new enterprise he has begun with Wisdom/Work. Tom and Wisdom/Work were the first and only press I approached with this book of poetry. So I was immensely gratified that they agreed to publish it. Many thanks to all those associated with Wisdom/Work, especially Abigail Chiaramonte, who designed the book and made it look so attractive.

The Books of Wisdom/Work

Wisdom/Work is a new cooperative, cutting edge imprint and resource for publishing books by practical philosophers and innovative thinkers who can have a positive cultural impact in our time. We turn the procedures of traditional publishing upside down and put more power, a vastly higher speed of delivery, and greater rewards into the hands of our authors.

The imprint was launched with the Morris Institute for Human Values, founded by Tom Morris (Ph.D. Yale), a former professor of philosophy at Notre Dame and a public philosopher who has given over a thousand talks on the wisdom of the ages. Wisdom/Work was established to serve both his audiences and the broader culture. From the imprint's first projects, it began to attract the attention of other authors who seek to expand their positive influence.

Wisdom/Work occupies a distinctive territory outside most traditional publishing domains. Its main concern is high quality expedited production and release, with affordability for buyers. We seek to serve a broad audience of intelligent readers with the best of ancient and modern wisdom. Subjects will touch on such issues as success, ethics, happiness, meaning, work, and how best to live a good life.

As an imprint, we have created a process for working with a few high quality projects a year compatible with our position in the market, and making available to our authors a well-guided and streamlined process for launching their books into the world. For more information, email Tom Morris, Editor-in-Chief, through his reliable address of: TomVMorris@aol.com. You can also learn more at the editor's website, www.TomVMorris.com.

Made in the USA
Columbia, SC
02 November 2021